SURVIVAL CHALLENGE

LOST!

Could YOU find your way in the world's wildest places?

STEPHANIE TURNBULL

A+

Smart Apple Media

Published by Smart Apple Media,
an imprint of Black Rabbit Books
P.O. Box 3263, Mankato, Minnesota, 56002
www.blackrabbitbooks.com

Designed and illustrated by Guy Callaby
Edited by Mary-Jane Wilkins

Cataloging-in-Publication Data is available from the Library of Congress

ISBN 978-1-62588-216-5

Photo acknowledgements
t = top; c = center; b = bottom
    folio image iStockphoto/Thinkstock; page 2 iStockphoto/
    Thinkstock; 3 Jupiterimages/Thinkstock; 4 Galyna
    Andrushko/Shutterstock; 5t Sinseeho/Shutterstock,
    c Sam DCruz, b Tyler Olson/all Shutterstock;
    6 auremar/Shutterstock; 7 John McLaird/
    Shutterstock; 8t AVAVA, c Kokhanchikov, b terekhov
    igor/Shutterstock; 12 Kotenko Oleksandr, b vrihu/
    Shutterstock; 14t Eduardo Rivero, b iStockphoto/
    Thinkstock; 15t Pietus, b Anatoliy Lukich/both Shutterstock;
    16 Yuriy Kulik/Shutterstock; 18 Roberto Caucino/Shutterstock;
19 Fedorov Oleksiy/Shutterstock; 20 fivespots/Shutterstock; 21t Florin Stana,
b auremar/both Shutterstock; 23 iStock/Thinkstock
Cover iStock/Thinkstock

Printed in China

DAD0056
032014
9 8 7 6 5 4 3 2 1

CONTENTS

TAKE THE CHALLENGE

Imagine you're an intrepid explorer trekking through deep jungle, wild woodland, misty mountains or icy Arctic wastes.

It's been a long, grueling day and you're exhausted. Surely it shouldn't take this long to reach camp?

You stop dead and look around with growing panic. The horrible truth sinks in: you're lost in the wilderness. **Your challenge is to get out alive. Can you do it?**

In the vast desert, empty sand dunes stretch out endlessly and the sun beats down mercilessly.

4

Dense, dripping trees and bushes tower over you in the steamy rainforest, blocking out the light.

It's hard to know where to turn when you're surrounded by steep, crumbling cliffs.

On the desolate Arctic plains it's so windy you can hardly lift your head to look around.

5

CHECK YOUR MAP

No explorer sets out without a map. Now's the time to look at yours. Maps show lots of information, but they're only useful if you have an idea where you are—which you don't. Before you give up, try these tricks.

FIND CLUES

Look around carefully. Can you spot any landmarks that might be drawn on the map, such as a hill, trail or river? Climb a tree or scramble up a rock to help you see further. Study the map, too—it might show something you remember passing earlier.

⬆ *Move around for different views of nearby features.*

USE CONTOURS

Your map has lines called contours. The closer together the **contours** are, the more steeply the ground rises. Compare the map with the shape of the land around you. Are there any steep hills or deep valleys?

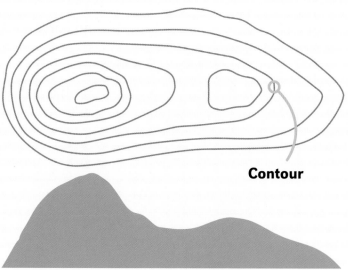

Contour

PLAN A ROUTE

If you find a landmark, turn the map in your hands until it matches the landscape. Find where your camp is on the map and plan a route. Start walking, but keep checking the map to see if it matches the land around you.

REAL LIFE SURVIVAL

In 2001, a student named Jason Rasmussen set off hiking along a trail in Minnesota. He had a map but didn't use it as the trail looked easy to follow. But after a few hours it ended and Jason realized he must have taken a wrong turn. He studied his map but couldn't work out where he was. He spent seven days alone in the wild before being rescued. He should have checked his map earlier!

GET YOUR BEARINGS

What if your map is lost, or useless, or eaten by wild animals? Don't panic. Can you work out which direction you're facing? The best way to do this is with a compass.

HOW A COMPASS WORKS

A compass has a magnetic needle sealed in a liquid-filled case. Because the Earth is like a huge magnet, it pulls anything magnetic to line up with the **North Pole** and **South Pole**. The red end of the needle points north, so the other end points south.

Compasses work anywhere in the world, in all weathers. You can even see the needle in the dark because it's luminous.

FIND NORTH

Hold your compass level and still. The needle should swing to north. You can then turn the dial so that the 'N' for north lines up with the needle.

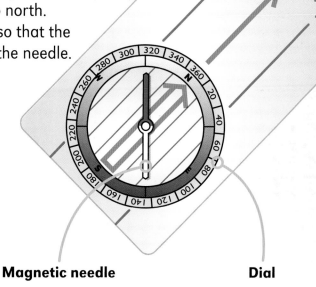

Magnetic needle   **Dial**

Once you know which direction you're facing, you may have a better idea where to head. Check the compass as you walk to make sure you don't go round in circles!

A famous Arctic explorer named Roald Amundsen was trying to sail his ship through a narrow channel full of drifting ice, when disaster struck— his compass needle broke. It was too foggy to see, so the crew had to let the ship float on and just hope they didn't hit ice. Luckily they made it safely through to open sea.

REAL LIFE SURVIVAL

MAKE A COMPASS

Perhaps you fell down a ridge and smashed your compass, or it was swept away in a river. Don't waste time: find the tools to make your own!

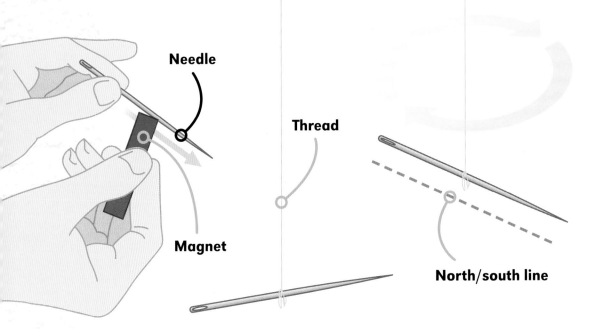

Needle

Thread

Magnet

North/south line

1. Find a magnet and a small metal object, such as a needle. Rub the needle in one direction against a magnet for 30 seconds to make it magnetic.

2. Find a piece of thread (you could pull a piece from your clothes) and tie it around the middle of the needle. Hang it so the needle can turn freely.

3. The magnetized needle will swing round to align with north and south. Which is which? Find out with an **analog watch**.

Eric LeMarque got lost while snowboarding in the Sierra Nevada Mountains. He had no compass so he made his own, which showed him that he was heading in the wrong direction. He set off for home and was rescued seven days later—frostbitten but alive.

REAL LIFE SURVIVAL

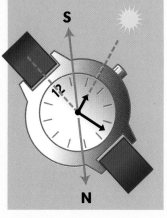

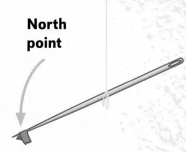

North point

4. *If you're in the* **northern hemisphere,** *point the hour hand of the watch at the sun.*

5. *Find 12 o'clock on the watch. Imagine a line halfway between the hour hand and 12 o'clock. This is south... so the opposite direction is north.*

6. *Look at your needle compass again. Stick something on the north point to remind you which way is which.*

7. *In the* **southern hemisphere,** *point the 12 o'clock position at the sun. Imagine a line between 12 o'clock and the hour hand to find south.*

11

USE THE SUN

You can use the sun to work out directions (unless you're in thick fog or lost at night). Ancient explorers used it long before maps and compasses were invented!

THE SUN'S PATH

Wherever you are in the world, the sun rises in the east and sets in the west. So if it's getting late and the sun is low in the sky, walking towards it means you're heading west.

Tami Oldham Ashcraft was sailing in the Pacific Ocean when a tropical storm ruined her navigation equipment. She was left drifting helplessly at sea. Fortunately she had a machine

called a **sextant**, so she could calculate her position using the sun. She used this to plot her route and reached land 42 days later.

REAL LIFE SURVIVAL

LOOK AT SHADOWS

Here's a clever way to work out basic compass points using the sun.

1. *Find some flat ground in full sun. Push a stick upright in the ground.*

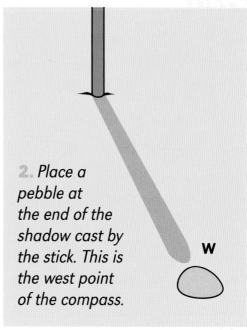

2. *Place a pebble at the end of the shadow cast by the stick. This is the west point of the compass.*

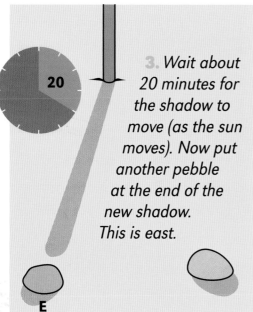

3. *Wait about 20 minutes for the shadow to move (as the sun moves). Now put another pebble at the end of the new shadow. This is east.*

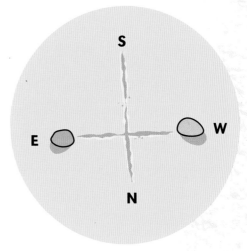

4. Mark a line in the ground linking the two pebbles, and another through the middle of it to show north and south.

13

THINK NATURAL

Ancient explorers knew that plants, animals and weather have regular patterns, so they learned to read these signs. Follow their example and pay attention to the natural world around you.

WATCH THE WIND

Most places have a prevailing wind, which means a direction the wind usually blows from. Over time, trees in windswept places lean away from it. So if you know the usual wind direction, look for leaning trees to act as pointers.

If the prevailing wind here is from the north, these branches are pointing south.

North American compass plants are tall and look rather like sunflowers.

LOOK AT PLANTS

Plants can be useful, too. The North American compass plant has leaves that almost always face north and south. They do this to avoid the hot noon sun.

14

SPOT SOME MOSS

Moss grows in shade, so in the northern hemisphere it often covers the north side of rocks and trees (and the south side in the southern hemisphere). But beware—it grows so fast that it may cover whole tree trunks!

> ➲ *Where there's a lot of moss, look for the thickest patches.*

COPY ANIMALS

Wild animals don't get lost! Flocks of birds often **migrate** south in winter and north in spring, crossing whole countries and oceans on the way.

> ➲ *Monarch butterflies fly from Canada to Mexico to lay eggs in winter. New butterflies return north in summer.*

Polynesian sailors have always been skilled at finding their way using the patterns of waves. One famous navigator was Mau Piailug, who in 1976 decided to sail from Hawaii to Tahiti using just the waves, sun, moon and wind to work out directions. It took a whole month, but he did it!

REAL LIFE SURVIVAL

LOOK AT STARS

So it's night time and you're *still* lost. Things may look bad, but you can try another ancient skill—using the stars to navigate.

THE NORTH STAR

In the northern hemisphere, one very bright star can help you get your bearings. This is the North Star and it's always above the North Pole. Here's how to find it.

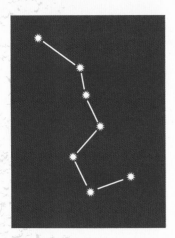

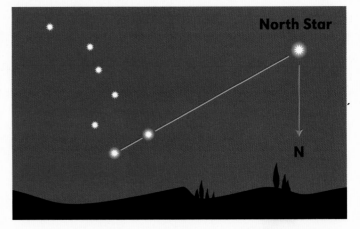

North Star

N

1. *Look for a* **constellation** *of stars called the Big Dipper. Imagine a line joining them, in the shape of a plough, or in the shape of a cup with a long handle.*

2. *Now concentrate on the two bright stars at the end of the cup. Extend the imaginary line until it reaches another star. This is the North Star, and directly below it is north.*

Look for a landmark to help you remember the direction. When you're facing it, you know that south is behind you, east is right and west is left.

16

THE SOUTHERN CROSS

The southern hemisphere doesn't have a handy star pointing south, but it does have a useful group of five stars called the Southern Cross.

1. Imagine a cross shape linking the four brightest stars.

2. Now imagine the line extending down, four and a half times the length of the cross.

3. Look directly below the end of the line. This is south.

1

2

3

4

4½

S

Dan Stephens was hiking in woods in Minnesota when he fell and knocked himself out. When he awoke he was so dazed and confused that he got completely lost. Soon night fell, but fortunately he knew how to navigate using the stars. Three days later he made it back to camp.

REAL LIFE SURVIVAL

GET A GADGET

You can save time and worry in the wild by carrying a high-tech phone or GPS receiver to check your location or even call for help.

REAL LIFE SURVIVAL

In 1986, French explorer Jean-Louis Etienne set out from northern Canada to reach the North Pole on foot. He carried a radio transmitter that sent signals via satellite to friends in France. They tracked his position and sent him directions. After 63 days of walking he reached the North Pole. The system had worked!

HOW GPS WORKS

GPS stands for Global Positioning System. There are 24 GPS **satellites** in space, each traveling around the Earth on its own fixed path, sending out signals.

A receiver picks up signals from the nearest four satellites. It times how long the signals take to arrive and calculates its position on the Earth's surface.

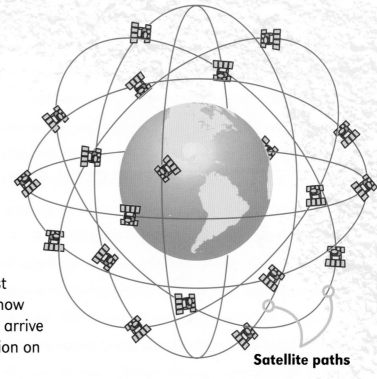

Satellite paths

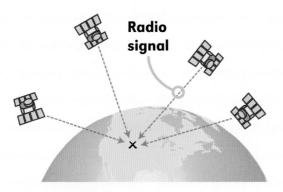

Radio signal

GPS receivers can give you a **grid reference** to check on a map. Most readings are accurate to around 33 feet (10m). That's pretty impressive!

BUT REMEMBER ...

Never rely totally on technology. Batteries run out quickly (especially in cold weather) and tall trees or other obstacles can block satellite signals from reaching you. And what if you drop and break your precious gadget, or lose it in a blizzard or sandstorm?

USE YOUR HEAD

So you think you know which way to go? Stop and think first. Is this the best plan or could it lead you into greater danger? Don't start off until you're sure.

MIND YOUR STEP!

Check your map, compass or GPS regularly, but look where you're going, too! Are you on a cliff edge or near a murky swamp? Watch for animal tracks. If you disturb a bear, snake or crocodile, being lost may be the least of your problems.

WATCH THE WEATHER

Keep an eye on the sky—are storm clouds gathering or is fog closing in? If so, find a shelter and wait for the weather to improve. Don't risk getting cold, drenched or struck by lightning.

LEARN LESSONS

When you make it to safety, learn from your mistakes. Plan your next trip better and follow your route carefully. Take the right equipment and make sure you know how to use it. And don't go alone!

GLOSSARY

analog watch
A watch with hands that show the time, not a digital display.

constellation
A group of stars that form a pattern.

contours
Lines on a map that link land of identical height.

grid reference
A set of numbers to check against numbered lines down and across your map to find a location.

migrate
To move to a different place to live.

northern hemisphere
The northern half of the world. It is separated from the southern hemisphere by an imaginary line around the middle of the world called the equator.

North Pole
The most northern point of the Earth. The North Pole on maps is in a slightly different position from the magnetic North Pole, where a compass arrow points.

satellite
An object that travels around a planet. Many satellites are built to do certain jobs, such as sending radio signals to GPS receivers.

sextant
A navigation tool with a telescope and measuring equipment. Sailors use it to find out where they are from the position of the sun, moon or stars above the horizon.

southern hemisphere
The southern half of the world. It is separated from the northern hemisphere by the equator.

South Pole
The most southern point of the Earth. The South Pole on maps is in a slightly different position from the magnetic South Pole.

www.wilderness-survival-skills.com/finding-direction.html
Tips on finding directions using ancient skills.

www.abc-of-hiking.com/navigation-skills
Useful facts and warnings to help you navigate in the wild.

www.thesurvivalexpert.co.uk/SurvivalBasicsCategory.html
How to make a compass, use GPS and lots more vital survival advice.

INDEX